I0528988

Praise for *A Wheel of Ravens*

"This is the work of a master craftsman, the owner of a true word hoard which he freely unlocks. We are led as a result into a world that is very much that of the Old North, in which the landscapes are of fjord and fen, mountain and moor, wood and wold. The winters are long and fierce, the summers fleeting and golden as youth. Upon this canvas move the full cast of primeval Germanic figures, human and divine, monstrous and alluring, remote and all too intrusive. The verse in which they interact is wrought as finely as a Dark Age sword, made for action and performance and not merely for the glass case of a page. I have chosen already the selections that I shall recite myself around seasonal campfires. This living, glittering poetry is a true gift to the modern age."

— **Ronald Hutton**, Author of *Pagan Britain*

"Adam Bolivar's *A Wheel of Ravens*, containing his recent poems written in Old English alliterative verse, is a revelation. The skill and panache with which Bolivar has adapted this ancient verse form to the weird mode is exhilarating. We are thrust back into the Dark Ages of pagan gods and doughty warriors—but in their midst are witches, minstrels, dragons, and other baleful creatures. With every poem Bolivar casts a mystic rune that lures the reader into his primitive but fascinating world."

— **S. T. Joshi**, Editor of *Spectral Realms*

"This book must be one of the single most original books that I have read. . . . How far are we from the Olympus created by the Mediterranean Sea and its culture. Welcome, dear reader, to a novel world!"

— **Donald Sidney-Fryer**, Author of
The Atlantis Fragments

Praise for *The Ettinfell of Beacon Hill*

"An inventive and ambitious fusion of supernatural investigations, folk myths, nursery rhymes and fairy tales—with even a touch of the Biblical and the Mythosian. This is the line of Jack the Bold and Jack the Cursed, flickering between England and New England, flitting across the centuries, to achieve strange resolutions. Imaginative, enjoyable, and cunningly constructed."

— **John Linwood Grant**, Author of
Where All is Night, and Starless

"Boston has never been an unhaunted city, but with the occult investigations of John Drake, Adam Bolivar infuses the psychogeography of New England with the balladry of old weird Britain to darkly humorous, decadently erudite, and dependably ingenious effect."

— **Sonya Taaffe**, Author of *Forget the Sleepless Shores*

"In *The Ettinfell of Beacon Hill*, Adam Bolivar is your guide through the gaslit streets of Boston, where impossibly erudite men battle back against the forces of darkness. With echoes of Wellman and Lovecraft, this collection of intertwined tales is a must-read for lovers of the dark fantastical Weird."

— **Matthew M. Bartlett**, Author of
Gateways to Abomination

"Atmospheric and eerie, the twelve gothic tales in *The Ettinfell of Beacon Hill* are diminutive period pieces: interlaced, twined by literary tradition, yet independently admirable, not only reminding readers of Adam Bolivar's prowess as a poet, but his savvy as a storyteller."

— **Clint Smith**, Author of *The Skeleton Melodies*

Also by Adam Bolivar

The Lay of Old Hex: Spectral Ballads & Weird Jack Tales

Ballads for the Witching Hour

The Ettinfell of Beacon Hill: Gothic Tales of Boston

The Wyrd of the Ettinfell (forthcoming)

Poetry from Jackanapes Press

Past the Glad and Sunlit Season: Poems for Halloween
by K. A. Opperman / Illustrated by Dan Sauer

October Ghosts and Autumn Dreams: More Poems for Halloween
by K. A. Opperman / Illustrated by Dan Sauer

The Withering: Poems of Supernatural Horror
by Ashley Dioses / Illustrated by Mutartis Boswell

The Voice of the Burning House
by John Shirley / Illustrated by Dan Sauer

Book of Shadows: Grim Tales and Gothic Fancies
by Manuel Arenas / Illustrated by Dan Sauer

*Not a Princess, but (Yes) There was a Pea and
other Fairy Tales to Foment Revolution*
by Rebecca Buchanan

I Awaken in October: Poems of Folk Horror and Halloween
by Scott J. Couturier / Illustrated by Dan Sauer

Halloween Hearts
by Adele Gardner

Darkest Days and Haunted Ways
by Ashley Dioses

www.JackanapesPress.com
www.facebook.com/Jackanapes-Press

A WHEEL OF RAVENS

Hræfna Hwéol

ᚺᚱᚨᚹᚾᚨᛋ · ᚺᚹᛖᛖᛚ

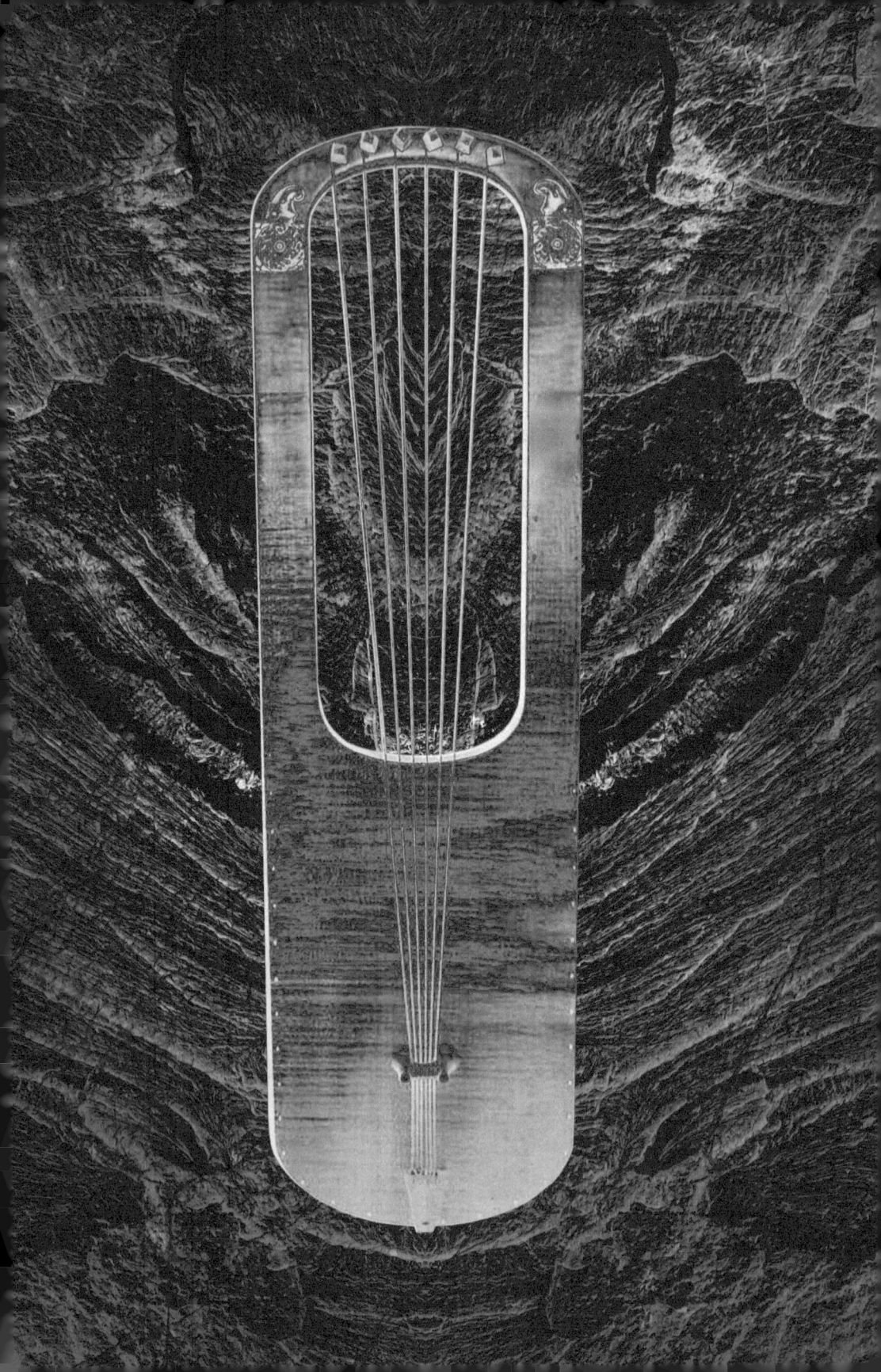

A WHEEL OF RAVENS

Hræfna Hwéol

ᚢᚱᚪᚠᛏᚠ · ᚢᚹᛖᛗᛏ

Alliterative Verse
in the Old English Style

Adam Bolivar

Foreword by Dennis Wilson Wise

JACKANAPES
PRESS

A Wheel of Ravens
Copyright © 2023 by Jackanapes Press. All rights reserved.
www.JackanapesPress.com

All poems and Introductiuon copyright © 2023 by Adam Bolivar
Foreword copyright © 2023 by Dennis Wilson Wise
Cover art and title page art copyright © 2023 by Daniel V. Sauer

Detailed information on the images used in this book can be found on
pages 109-110, which form an extension of this copyright page.

Cover and interior design by Dan Sauer
www.DanSauerDesign.com

First Paperback Edition

1 3 5 7 9 8 6 4 2

ISBN: 978-1-956702-10-1

All characters and other entities appearing in this work are fictitious or are used in a fictitious way. Any
resemblance to real persons, dead or alive, or other real-life entities, past or present, is purely coincidental.

All rights reserved. No part of this work may be reproduced in any form or by any means without the
written permission of the publisher, except in the case of brief quotations embodied in reviews.

For fairest Fríg,
most fascinating of goddesses

Contents

FOREWORD

THE BOOK YOU'RE HOLDING, *A Wheel of Ravens*, is
a special one. For one thing, it's the first collection of
original short verse written entirely in an alliterative style.
For another, it's our first book written by a poet who
fully recognizes the Modern Alliterative Revival *as* a
major literary movement. My correspondence with Adam
began back in June 2021 after a mutual acquaintance,
Frank Coffman, the horror poet, saw a CfP I'd posted
for my critical anthology, *Speculative Poetry and the
Modern Alliterative Revival*, on the Facebook page for
the SFPA. He told me about this one writer he knew,
a contemporary balladeer interested strongly in formal
verse. Well, I contacted Adam that same afternoon,
but, unfortunately, his ready-at-hand poems were all
in traditional accentual-syllabic meters—the natural
category, of course, for ballads. Still, Bolivar expressed
an interest in the medieval alliterative form, so I asked if
he'd be interested in an original contribution. He was.
Some weeks later he submitted a draft for "The Lay of

Gēac Ettin-Fell," a compilation of several "Jack Tales" in Old English meter. After some workshopping I accepted the poem and, normally, that would have concluded our correspondence. But a seed had been planted. About a year later, out of the blue, Adam contacted me again. In the meantime he'd written an entire collection of alliterative verse—the book you're holding, *A Wheel of Ravens*—and could I perhaps write a blurb or even a foreword? Given how closely this volume intersects with my own research, I naturally jumped at the chance—and the rest, as they say, is history.

Still, history can be a funny thing. As I read through *A Wheel of Ravens*, I came to realize that not only had Bolivar written a *special* book—he'd written a remarkable one as well. It is a collection, as Bolivar writes in his introduction, about the "pre-Christian English" people. For anyone familiar with early medieval history, this reference links the story-content in Bolivar's texts to a very narrow historical window, the "dark" years following Rome's withdrawal from Britain in the early fifth century. This withdrawal—an abandonment, actually—left the native Britons, a highly Romanized and therefore Christian people—the late empire having officially converted a century earlier—to fend for themselves. According to the Venerable Bede in his *Ecclesiastical History of the English People* (completed 731 AD), these Britons, under threat by the Picts from the north, in the late 440s decided to invite several Germanic tribes from northern Europe to settle. While these tribes—the Angles, the Saxons, the Jutes—did, indeed, offer the Britons some early protection, a later dispute also led them to ally *with* the Picts *against* the Britons, resulting in disaster for the latter. From that point forward, these Christianized Britons retreated to modern-day Wales and Cornwall, and the Anglo-Saxon heptarchy arose in modern-day England. These new Anglo-Saxon polities, however, were deeply pagan. True to their Germanic origins, they worshipped deities now best remembered by their Old Norse names: Odin (*Óðinn*), Thor (*Þórr*), Freya (*Fríg*), Loki, Baldur. Yet this pagan interlude lasted just a short while. In 597 AD, Pope Gregory of the Roman Church sent a mission of forty monks to the island; a few years later, King Æthelbert of Kent, encouraged probably by his Christian Frankish wife Bertha, became the first Anglo-Saxon monarch to adopt the new religion. Over the next century the British Isles would slowly re-Christianize, and this process would be mostly complete by around 700 AD.

So readers approaching *A Wheel of Ravens* like good historians should already know, logically, that Bolivar's stories hail from sometime within good, clear, historical time: the fifth, sixth, and seventh centuries AD. None of this *real* history, however, actually enters Bolivar's texts. Perhaps our closest reference occurs in "To Sing of the

Gods," a poem wherein "craven" Christians slay a hermit whose only crime lay in composing songs about old gods, though gods now associated with the Devil by a newly reigning Christian orthodoxy. In this context, readers may perhaps recall the passage from *Beowulf* where the Danes, desperate for relief against the murderous violence of Grendel, offer sacrifices at pagan shrines, an action censured by the *Beowulf*-poet. Notably, although *Beowulf*'s central events all occur in Scandinavia during the early sixth century, their pagan Heroic Age, our lone manuscript for *Beowulf* (not to mention most other surviving Old English manuscripts) all problematically hail from the *tenth* century. Considering how these Christian Anglo-Saxon writers and monks took quite dim views of their pagan antecedents—in stark contrast to their Icelandic counterparts, to whom we owe nearly all our knowledge about Norse mythology and paganism—there thus exists almost no literature *in* Old English that doesn't view the Early English people's pagan centuries through a hostile ideological lens.

Bolivar removes that filtering Christian viewpoint from *A Wheel of Ravens*, but, significantly, he removes concrete history as well: facts, dates, synods like the one at Whitby in 664, and the ecclesiastical and social politics of the fifth, sixth, and seventh centuries. Instead, *A Wheel of Ravens* follows the logic of "once upon a time"—the logic of folklore and fairy tales. Here, manuscripts such as *The Anglo-Saxon Chronicle* matter less than the remnants of story from our collective folk memory. None of Bolivar's poems are localizable to a specific year or decade. The figures who appear—Cyndraca, Dréamwulf, Randwulf, Ælfflæd—arise from neither historical legend (such as Hrothgar and Ingeld in *Beowulf*) nor accounts such as Bede's *Ecclesiastical History* but from an Old English folkloric tradition presented as authentic by Bolivar. For example, in "A Dragon Dreamt" we encounter this fiery mythological beast, the dragon, but, although this dragon had taken its treasure from "kingdoms / in an olden age when the earth was young," readers never learn whether this ancient kingdom was Roman Britain—a possibility—nor whether this dragon's desolation disrupted the reign of Hadrian, Constantine, or some other Roman emperor. Since fairy tales and folk tales always partake of timelessness, that is how we engage the stories in *A Wheel of Ravens*. Even geography belongs more to romance and fantasy than to reality. Every once in a while Bolivar will mention a proper name such as Cornwall or Devonshire, which affixes many of his tales to southwest Britain, but just as often we'll explore geographical realms found only within the wondrous neverwhere of Faërie: ettin-filled castles, a wicked woods, dreamland, Ælfhám.

Indeed, only one true event from real history explicitly enters *A Wheel of Ravens*, but even this event Bolivar treats as mythic: "Regneracu," aka Ragnarök. According to *The Elder Edda*, as many readers probably know, several major Norse deities—Odin, Tyr, Heimdall, and others—are destined to perish in one catastrophic final battle against Loki and the giants (*jötnar* in Old Norse, *eotenas* in Old English). The equivalent deities in pagan Anglo-Saxon England, of course, are doomed to suffer similar fates, but it's clear that *A Wheel of Ravens* is a post-Ragnarök collection of tales. For evidence look no further than Bolivar's first poem, "The Song of the Sword." Although we are told that the god Wóden (Odin) may be "fallen, faded, | and feared no longer," there yet survives a *wyrd*-wrought weapon—the eponymous sword wielded later by Cyndraca the Hero —that will wreck a "gruesome joy" from beyond the grave for those old Germanic deities. What Bolivar purports to do, then, is resurrect a "lost" tradition of pagan folklore and fairy tale in an authentic poetic form across one, great, *and historical* "Ragnarök." The Twilight of the Gods isn't a doom as yet unbefallen. Rather, it is nothing other than the quite real process of Christianization during the seventh century in the British Isles: the endpoint to a black hole in our collective folk memory and the real doom for the old Germanic gods in the English tradition.

No narrative thread in *A Wheel of Ravens* better articulates this theme than Cyndraca/Géac. Given Bolivar's long interest in Jack Tales—a cycle now best remembered through stories like "Jack and the Beanstalk," "Jack the Giant-killer," and the nursery rhyme "Jack and Jill"—we can see how *A Wheel of Ravens* attempts to grant this trickster-hero a much older medieval genealogy than he actually has. Notably, the adventures of Cyndraca recycle many elements common to Jack Tales. Boots of speed? Check. A cap of prophecy? Sure. Cloak of darkness? Certainly. Bolivar even ties his invented hero Cyndraca (and thus the later Jack) to other famous remnants of folklore and legend. Scholars have hypothesized one connection already between Jack and King Arthur, another famous giant-killer from Cornwall with associations with Merlin/Myrrdin, but, through Cyndraca, Bolivar posits another connection as well: Jack and the Dream Cycle of H. P. Lovecraft, whose great hero Randolph Carter—"Randwulf"—bears a silver key that unlocks the gates of dreamland.

Of course, the one historical hurdle that Bolivar sidesteps is that no Jack Tales were preserved in manuscript form until the fifteenth century, the tail-end of the Middle Ages. We know such tales, though, must have circulated orally long beforehand, so the Old English alliterative meter helps Bolivar tie these tales to the pagan culture of the Early English people. In other words, Bolivar follows modern fantasy's long tradition of creative reconstruction. Although Regneracu may have slain the old Germanic deities, Cyndraca escapes. Unlike other great warriors from Germanic heroic legend—Sigurd, Dietrich von Bern, others—Cyndraca contests with his *wyrd* ... and wins. He survives the Doom of the Gods, but he survives in changed cultural form, as Géac, a character more roguish, less grim, than his original, yet still a direct folkloric descendent nonetheless. Over time, Bolivar hints, natural linguistic evolution will eventually transform "Géac" (pronounced *yay*-ac in Old English) to "Jack."

Despite this ambitious literary conception that Bolivar realizes through his use of alliterative poetics, however, he wisely abandons other potential avenues of historical fidelity. No surviving manuscript in Old English, for example, utilizes the same "cycle of poems" format as *A Wheel of Ravens*—clearly, a modern way of imagining a poetry collection. Likewise, Old English verse usually falls into one of four categories: the heroic, the elegiac, the gnomic, and the ecclesiastical or religious. Only one of those categories, the gnomic, which includes riddles, appears unambiguously within *A Wheel of Ravens*. Otherwise, the fairy-tale elements in Bolivar's collection are highly anachronistic for the fifth, sixth, and seventh centuries, although it must be said that no less an authority than J. R. R. Tolkien once wrote a fairy-tale pastiche of *Beowulf* based on what he considered its lost "fairy tale" elements. This pastiche he called "Sellic Spell," a name taken from the phrase *syllíc spell* in

Beowulf meaning a "strange or wondrous tale." In that sense, then, *A Wheel of Ravens* is best viewed as a collection of wonder tales. In the guise of "preserving" an authentically pagan English folklore, Bolivar creates an esteemed literary prehistory for modern-day Jack Tales. It is this unique blend of medieval and modern that makes Bolivar's volume such a fascinating collection. If the Modern Alliterative Revival will continue flourishing as a movement, then it needs more books like *A Wheel of Ravens*—more poets like Bolivar—willing to exploit the thematic and metrical possibilities of alliterative meter in modern speculative poetry.

Dennis Wilson Wise
University of Arizona
Tucson, Arizona

Introduction

Alliterative verse was the traditional form of Germanic poetry from antiquity through much of the Middle Ages. It is found in Old English poems such as *Beowulf*, as well as Old Norse sagas and the *Poetic Edda* of the Icelanders. In early mediæval (5th- to 11th-century) England, a *scop* (the counterpart of the Norse *skáld*) would recite or sing these poems while strumming a distinctive lyre called a *hearpe*, shaped like a long rectangle with rounded ends and with an opening in the upper section across which sheep-gut strings were stretched. Thus, the poetry of the *scop* was *scopcræft*.

This venerable art is now all but forgotten by English-speakers. Brought to Britain in the fifth century by the precursors of the English—migrant tribes of Angles, Saxons and Jutes from what is now Denmark, northern Germany and the Netherlands—it was supplanted by the rhyming poetry imported by the French-speaking Normans after their conquest of England in 1066. The Anglo-Saxon lyre was banned as a symbol of nativist anti-Norman sentiment, and alliteration fell from fashion. Alliterative verse, albeit of an altered kind, nevertheless persisted, and enjoyed a brief revival in the 14th century in the North and the West Midlands of England and in Scotland, although it was derided as uncultivated in the South. (In Chaucer's *Canterbury Tales*, the Parson, a Southerner, mocks alliteration as *rum ram ruf.*) It is high time to restore dignity to this noble and neglected form.

Here are the rules of Old English alliterative verse that I have adopted in my own poems:

- Each line is broken into two half-lines—the on-verse and the off-verse—separated by a break called a cæsura.

- Each half-line (which consists of a minimum of four syllables) has two stressed syllables.

- The first stressed syllable in the off-verse must alliterate with one of the stressed syllables in the on-verse. The remaining stressed syllable in the on-verse can also alliterate with the others but is not required to. The second stressed syllable in the off-verse must *not* alliterate.

- The term 'alliteration' is something of a misnomer. It is the *sound* that must be repeated, not the letter: 'king' can alliterate with 'cat' and 'feather' with 'phoenix'. As such, 'ch', 'sh' and 'th' sounds must alliterate (so to speak).

- While it often is, the stressed alliterated syllable does not have to be at the beginning of the word. The 'en**chan**ted **child**' is a valid construction.

- 'St' and 'sp' are required to alliterate. In Old English, so does 'sc', but since 'sc' is pronounced as the modern 'sh', I have not required 'sc' to alliterate in my Modern English poetry (although 'sh' must, as I have stated).

- All vowels may alliterate. 'Old' can alliterate with 'age', 'ice' with 'earth' and 'uncle' with 'Ælfric'.

- The rules governing the metre of alliterative verse are complex and I will not attempt to lay them out in their entirety. Simply put, there must be four metrical positions in each half-line: two lifts (heavily stressed syllables) and two dips (unaccented or weakly stressed syllables). Two consecutive stressed syllables are counted as separate lifts, but two or more adjoining unaccented or weakly accented syllables merge into a single dip. Thus, only certain combinations of lifts and dips are permissible to ensure that the four metrical positions are maintained. (The permitted combinations are called Sievers types, after the 19th-century German philologist who discovered them.)

My intention in writing these poems was to revive and celebrate the Old English form of alliterative verse in particular. As such, I have used the Old English names for mythological entities now better known by their Norse appellations: Wóden instead of Odin, Thunor rather than Thor, Hámdæl in place of Heimdall, and so forth. Because of a scarcity of written sources (due largely to deliberate suppression by Christians), many of the Old English names have been lost. However, since Old English and Old Norse are closely related languages, it is possible by means of cognates to reconstruct what the names might have been: for example, Loki may have been Lúca in Old English, and the fateful battle of *Ragnarök* could have been *Regneracu*.

It is known that the pre-Christian English broadly worshipped the same gods as their Scandinavian cousins, but whether their myths included all the same characters and details is unprovable. There are some tantalising hints however, such as Freyja's necklace *Brísingamen* appearing in *Beowulf* as *Brósinga mene,* the archaeological discovery of hammer of Thunor pendants in a sixth-century

14

Jutish cemetery in Kent, and a sixth-century buckle depicting Wodan (as he was known in Old Saxon) as one-eyed, unearthed in northern Germany, the homeland of the Saxons. And doubtless there was cultural exchange between the various Germanic tribes: Beowulf himself was a Geat from southern Sweden who came to Denmark, and whose story was carried to Britain by the Angles. In any event, this book is a work of fantasy—as a poet, I am free to let my imagination wander unfettered. Pray do not mistake my flights of fancy for strict scholarship. There is much about the tales and beliefs of the early English we may never know, save in poetry and dreams.

Adam Bolivar
Portland, Oregon, Western Wínland
Géolmonaþ (Yule-month), 2022

Wyrd biŏ ful aræd.

(The Wyrd is inexorable.)

— *The Wanderer,*
Old English poem

·|·

The Song of the Sword

The Song of the Sword   is sorrowful to hear;
By fate it was forged,   a fear-bringer,
Held by heroes,   its hilt graven
With runes of ruin,   the wrack of ettins,
A thirsty thorn   that threatens doom.
Who holds its hilt   will hear a song:
The wail of Wóden,   the woe of gods,
Fallen, faded,   and feared no longer.
But still the sword   slays their enemies,
Its blade blackened   by blood spilling
On ravening runes,   restlessly feeding,
And giving the gods   a gruesome joy.

· II ·

The Wyrd Sisters

Wise are the sisters,   the witches who bend,
And cast their spells   as a cat watches.
Threefold they huddle,   these throwers of runes,
Carefully carven   with the course of the wyrd,
While all on earth,   and over and below it,
Defer to their fingers,   furiously shaping
The lives of lords   alike with their thralls.
Few will find them,   fewer sway them,
Who pick the past,   present and future.
Old and eerie,   by an ash's roots,
The women wait   by the well of being,
Like the claws of the cat   the cut of their knives,
For everything ends,   even Wælheall.

A Vampyre of the Fens

In the fickle fens,   far from merriment,
Mirthful music,   and the mead-hall's warmth,
Lay a lonely   lurker in shadows,
A thrall to thirst,   a threat to life,
A stealthy strider,   stalking quarry
To drag to his den,   this drinker of blood,
A boon bringing   a brief respite
From deathless doom,   the undying curse
Of Cain's kindred,   the creatures of night.
A hero hunted,   his heart valorous,
An armoured earl,   an ettin-slayer,
Who found his foe   fleeing from daylight,
And hewed his head   with honed iron,
Fearlessly felling   the fen-vampyre.

· IIII ·

Darkness Fell

Brightest Bældæg   forbore the darts
Hurled at him heartily   by heroes and gods
Merrily met there,   no malice in their hearts,
For each object   was oathbound not to harm
The golden god   who gamely stood.
A blind man bore   a bolt in his hand,
Which a guileful god   guided carefully
So the spear would strike,   a spike in the heart
Made of mistletoe,   lamentably overlooked—
The death of Bældæg!   Now darkness fell
Over the gods,   an omen of doom.

·ᚾ·

The Black Herald

A raven roused,   roosted on the masthead
Of a sailing ship,   shiny with hoarfrost,
And opened his eyes   at the hour of midnight,
Black and baleful,   boding disaster.
The sailors swung   their swords at the bird,
Rousing the raven's   wrath at the insult,
For Hyge his name,   hallowed of ravens.
On sable wings   he soared away,
The luckless louts   left to perish
When a kraken came   to crush their ship;
They drowned dreadfully,   a dinner for Rán.

· ᚾ ·

Fairest Fríg

My fairest Fríg!—   how flowing your locks,
How soft your fingers,   how sultry your eyes.
By cats you are carried   in a carriage of silver,
And falcon feathers   flutter you skyward.
The favoured fallen   may feast in your hall,
Your breast brightened   by Brósingamene,
Whose fanciful filigree   was fashioned by dwarfs,
And set with gems   of scarlet hue.
You lavish lovers   with a long embrace—
O, would that I were one!

· ᚾᛁᛁ ·

The Wild Hunt

Wayfaring Wóden,   wise in runecraft,
Father of frenzies,   friend to poets,
Hoary-bearded,   hanging a nineday,
By a spear wounded   and sparing an eye,
Swift his steed is,   slipping from peril,
His hunt is heard   on the heath at night,
His howling hounds   hurrying before him,
While the horns of Hel   are heard blaring,
The foolish fellows   following the huntsman,
Damned, undying,   and doomed to wander.

· ΛIII ·

Hréam's Reward

Thunor threatened   to throttle his maid,
Leering Lúca   who laughed at his gow n,
A daring dodge   to dupe Hréam
In his wish to wed   bewitching Fríg
As payment to replace   pilfered Striker,
The heavenly hammer   of the hero's lore.
At the altar, the ettin   offered Striker
As fee for Fríg,   a fair exchange,
And lifting the veil,   learned the deception:
The hammer's hit   a heavy kiss,
And Hel's embrace   was Hréam's reward.

Dréamwulf

Dréamwulf Draca,   of Defenascír,
Was a skillful scop   besung in that country.
He happened on Fríg   in a hallowed place
One March morning,   in mist weeping.
The goddess gave him   a gift beyond measure,
A lilting lyre   alluring to all,
Strings softening   the strongest of wills,
But the price he paid   for this precious boon
Was bringing back   Brósingamene,
Steathily stolen   as a sting to Fríg.
From Wessex he walked,   wandering yonder,
His mournful music   melting indifference,
And lingering at length   in the land of Angles,
Where his music made   a mighty friend,
A worthy Wícing,   in warcraft versed.
Gnarr his name was   and known his blade.
The two travelled   on tricksome waters,
Over the ocean   after the necklace,
To Iceland, Greenland,   ever further,
The lyre leading them,   luring them onward
To Wínland, the widest   Wícingas had voyaged.
Dréamwulf and Gnarr   were driven south
To a hidden harbour   where a hill arose,
A secret sanctuary   where a serpent tarried.

Lúca laughed well   to look on these men
Who tried to take   his treasure away,
But the lyre lulled him   to lose his prize.
They dragged Lúca,   drowsing soundly
In enchanted chains   to a chamber in the hill
To sleep centuries,   a slave to his wyrd.

·ᚤ·

Mothers' Night

When the year circles   and Yule is nigh,
We meet in murk   for Mothers' Night,
Our offerings honouring   ancestresses prior.
Wolves are wailing   in the wilds beyond
As we slaughter swine   at the sacred place,
Their blood bathing   the blessing stone;
May fertile Fríg   favour our sacrifice,
And make mothers   of our maiden daughters.
Night is nascent   with new creation,
Her widened womb   waiting to engender
The dazzling dawn,   the day of wonder,
When Sunne sings,   sundered from thralldom.

· ᛁ ·

Heolstor

Unholy Heolstor,   in Hel an earl,
An occult ettin,   the offspring of Night,
Was dark, doomful   and dreadful to see.
He haunted the heath,   hated by shepherds,
And flaying flesh   from fools he met,
Their sorry screams   resounding far,
Weighty warnings   the wise heeded.
Cyndraca was summoned,   the cunning man,
Whose sword had slain   seven ettins,
His feats famous   both far and wide.
On the way a wizard,   one-eyed and hoary,
Gave him a lantern   engraved with runes
To drive out the darkness   bedevilling the land.
Cyndraca journeyed   to the cold wasteland,
Murky and misty   and moss covered,
And held up high   the hallowed lamp,
To find his foe   flat in heather,
Asleep, unseen,   obscured by a cloak,
But the lantern's light   left him exposed.
Quickly Cyndraca   killed Heolstor
By hewing the head   of the horrid ettin;
In the bounty of blood   his blade revelled.
Cyndraca secured   the cloak of Night,
A blessing in battle   and boon to thieves.

· ᚢᛁᛁ ·

On Winterfylleth

On Winterfylleth   the witches met
To dance drunkenly   on the darkened moor
By standing stones,   strange and ancient.
A bonfire blazed,   bright and merry,
And Lúca laughed,   unleashed that night
To frolic feral   and free from bonds
With mead-mad maids   ere morning came
To slink sulkily   to his silent vault.
Cunning Cyndraca   quickened thereafter,
A sly scion   to the slippery god,
Finding fortune   felling ettins
And gaining gold,   made glad by fame.

· ᚣᛁᛁᛁ ·

Hel Unloosed

To the horn hearken,   for Hámdæl blows!
The last of the light   which lingers in the world
Now falters and fades,   and fear prevails,
For dwelling in darkness   are dire monsters:
Ettins and ogres,   imps and púcas
Who hunch in holes—   all Hel is unleashed!
Wyrms are wending   their way upwards,
And Lúca leads them,   lusting for vengeance
Against the gods,   gloating at their downfall,
As Sunne slips   from her sky furrow,
And Móna moans   his matching end.
A witch told Wóden   his wyrd would bring
Woeful withering   in wolfish jaws;
In her runes she read   the ruin of Ósgeard.

My Name is Known

My name is known   near and yonder,
My wit a weapon   I wield with flash,
Readily routing   my rivals with a sword
Engraved with runes   of a grim future,
A warrior's wyrd   woven in the metal.
Ravens recount   the conquests I make
To wise Wóden,   who watches my feats,
Giving guidance   and gifts to use,
Ancient and elven,   inexorable in battle,
While kept in a cavern,   my kindred writhes,
The origin of my art   and author of my doom.

· ᚤᚾ ·

Cyndraca and the Wyrm

Cyndraca arrived   at a cursed barrow
Where a wyrm awoke   in a well's darkness,
Wriggling, writhing,   ravaging the valley,
Killing cattle,   carrying off children,
Feared by freemen,   a foul terror.
Fríg gave counsel   to favoured Cyndraca
To spike his armour   with spearheads of iron,
And fight this foe   by the flowing stream,
Then, serpent slain,   to slaughter whatever
Next he noticed   near the setting,
Lest his kindred carry   a curse in their blood.
Cyndraca clashed   with the cruel monster,
Its coils creeping   to crush his body,
A useless effort   on the armour's spikes.
His sword sundered   the serpent's head,
Which fell to his feet,   frothing vilely.
A cat was curious   of the corpse of the wyrm,
But Cyndraca cared not   to kill this darling,
And flouting the misfortune   befalling his heirs,
Would find friendship   with the feline race,
Whose aid he earned   often in future.

· ᚣᚾᛁ ·

Awful Eormenwyrm

Awful Eormenwyrm,   Ángnesboda's youngling
From lying with Lúca   the Lie-Father,
The Middangeard monster,   unmatched in size,
Which girdles the globe,   the greatest of serpents,
Tail extending   to entwine the earth,
Dreaded dweller   in the darkest sea.
Once Thunor threw   a thread from his boat,
The head of an ox   on a hook as bait,
And the slithering serpent   snapped at the morsel.
The hammer-heaver   hauled it to the surface,
Spitefully spitting   a spray of poison.
While steadying his stance   to strike with his hammer,
Thunor was thwarted   from thrashing the wyrm
By a craven companion   who cut the line,
And under the ocean   Eormenwyrm vanished.

Gnarled and Knotted

Gnarled and knotted,   never breaking,
Are the bitter bonds,   the bowels of his son,
Lashing Lúca   to lie on a stone,
A wyrm wiggling   towards his face,
Dripping upon it   drops of poison.
A spiteful smile   yet spreads his lips,
For at Regneracu   he will rise from his prison,
And blood will bathe   the blades of ettins,
As Lúca laughs   and leads his brethren
To right the wrongs   wreaked upon them
By arrogant gods   in ages past.

· ᚣᚾ|‖| ·

The Silver Key

Cyndraca clambered   up a cold mountain,
Desolate and distant   from Defenascír.
Here he happened   on a hoary sage,
Wizened Wóden,   one eye blazing,
Raucous ravens   roosting on his shoulders.
The god was gracious   and gave him a relic,
The silver key   sought by warlocks,
Granting entry   to the gate of dreams.
He kept the key   on a cord of leather;
It strained his slumbers   with strange visions
Of a dark tower,   dire and haunting,
Calling to Cyndraca   across the worlds,
From a cavern's core   the careful strumming
Of silver strings,   a silken voice
Enticing him, tempting him   to turn the key,
And earn ingress   to the ancient gate,
Swallowed by slumbers,   a swirling maelstrom,
To wander in a wood,   a wayfarer in dreams.

The Wanderers

Cyndraca followed   a footpath winding
Deeper and deeper   into a darkened wood.
He staggered by a stream,   strangely babbling,
Guiding him to a graveyard,   grey and haunted,
Where he met a man,   mannered and noble,
A traveller in dreams,   a treasure-seeker,
A creature of chaos,   crow-belovèd,
A renowned necromancer,   his name Randwulf,
His silver key   the same as Cyndraca's.
Warm was the meeting   of the wanderers here,
And into a tomb   trod the cohorts,
A secret stair   sloping downwards,
To a dark tunnel   by dwarfs burrowed,
Ushering them onwards   to an underground chamber.
In a box was a book,   bound in leather,
A hidden hoard   of Hel-runes within.
Randwulf revelled   in the rare knowledge,
Blind to the boggart   baring its talons.
Cyndraca dispatched   the creeping púca,
The head of the hob   hewn by his swordstroke,
Like flax falling   from a farmer's scythe.
On a parchment page   was a path to the tower,
But Randwulf's road   ran divergently,
So they parted ways,   promising friendship.

ᛯᚤᛯ

Emerald Éarendel

Emerald Éarendel, the eldest of stars,
Slipped from heaven and sank to earth,
Green and glowing, a beguiling gem,
Carried in the clutches of a crude ettin,
Bearing to his castle, the coveted hoard.
Learning this legend would lure Cyndraca,
The fierce fighter and feller of giants,
To the foetid fen where the fortress lay.
A conjurer's cloak keeping him shrouded,
Cyndraca went creeping through the cold fastness,
Stepping softly and stealing through the dark.
The ettin kept Éarendel in an oaken box,
His hands holding it as he heavily snored.
A sword sliced to sever his gullet,
Unwavering the stroke, the work of Cyndraca.
A glorious gift he gave to Fríg,
Emerald Éarendel, the eldest of stars,
And fortune followed the favoured earl
Across kingdoms, his conquests many.

· ᚤᚤᛁ ·

To Sing of the Gods

A hairy hermit   once hid in the fens;
In a ruin wreathed   in reeds he dwelt.
On fish he fed,   on fruit of the thorn;
He studied the sun,   the stars and the moon,
The day and the night   dancing like lovers.
He lifted his lyre   by the light of a fire,
Under silent skies   to sing of the gods
Who danced in his dreams,   adored of old:
First, trusty Tíw,   who traded his hand,
Then the Raven-God,   the rune-knower,
The Thunder-Maker,   who throws his hammer,
Fríg the fairest,   who fills with song,
And lying Lúca,   who is lashed in Hel.
Craven Christians   came with daggers
To deal a deathblow   to the dweller in the fens,
Whose lyrics lingered   for long afterwards,
Heard by poets   and heathen folk.

· ᚤᚤᚢᛁ ·

Wódnesmeolc

Now drink deeply,   you dreamers of songs,
Of the mystic mead,   the maker of poets,
Which Wóden the Wise   won by cunning.
To steal from a hoard   stored in a mountain.
As a snake he slipped   through a small tunnel,
And wooed the woman   watching the barrels;
He lay with the lady   who let him swallow
Some drinks of mead,   and his draughts were three,
Which emptied every   ounce of the supply.
He flew furiously   in the form of an eagle,
While the angry ettin   who owned the hoard
Also adopted   an eagle's shape
To fly after   fleeing Wóden,
Who spit out a stream,   a spate of mead
To vault the wall   warding Ósgeard,
Caught in barrels   carefully laid out,
Though drops dribbled   down to Middangeard,
The portion of poetasters,   the poor lackwits.

· ᚤᚤᛁᛁᛁ ·

Earth-stepping Ælfflæd

The singer sat   in a sorrowful ruin,
Far from the flowering   fields of her childhood.
With pale fingers   she plucked the strings
Of a lyre crafted   by Lúca himself,
The dark devil   who dwells in the earth.
Her fingers froze   from frost and chill,
But warm were the tears   this wanderess shed
Over crafty Cyndraca,   who called to her heart,
Earth-stepping Ælfflæd,   who ever trod
The elden path   once ettins had walked,
Her lyre leading her   through lands of dream.

· ᚤᚤᛁᛁ ·
A Lurid Lair

A crow attracted   Cyndraca's notice,
An ill omen   of an ettin nearby;
He pressed onwards   to perils ahead,
And found a field   foul with carnage.
His cloak of darkness   keeping him hidden,
Cyndraca crept through   a cave's opening
Into a lurid lair   littered with corpses,
The strong stench there   stifling his breathing.
A child was chained,   chilled with terror,
A morsel for the monster   who made this bloodshed.
The ettin entered,   angered at the trespass;
The invisible vanquisher   evaded his blows,
And sheared the shins   of the shouting ettin.
Cyndraca decapitated   the captor of the child,
Unbinding the boy   with a blow from his sword,
And granted him the gift   of a golden ring.

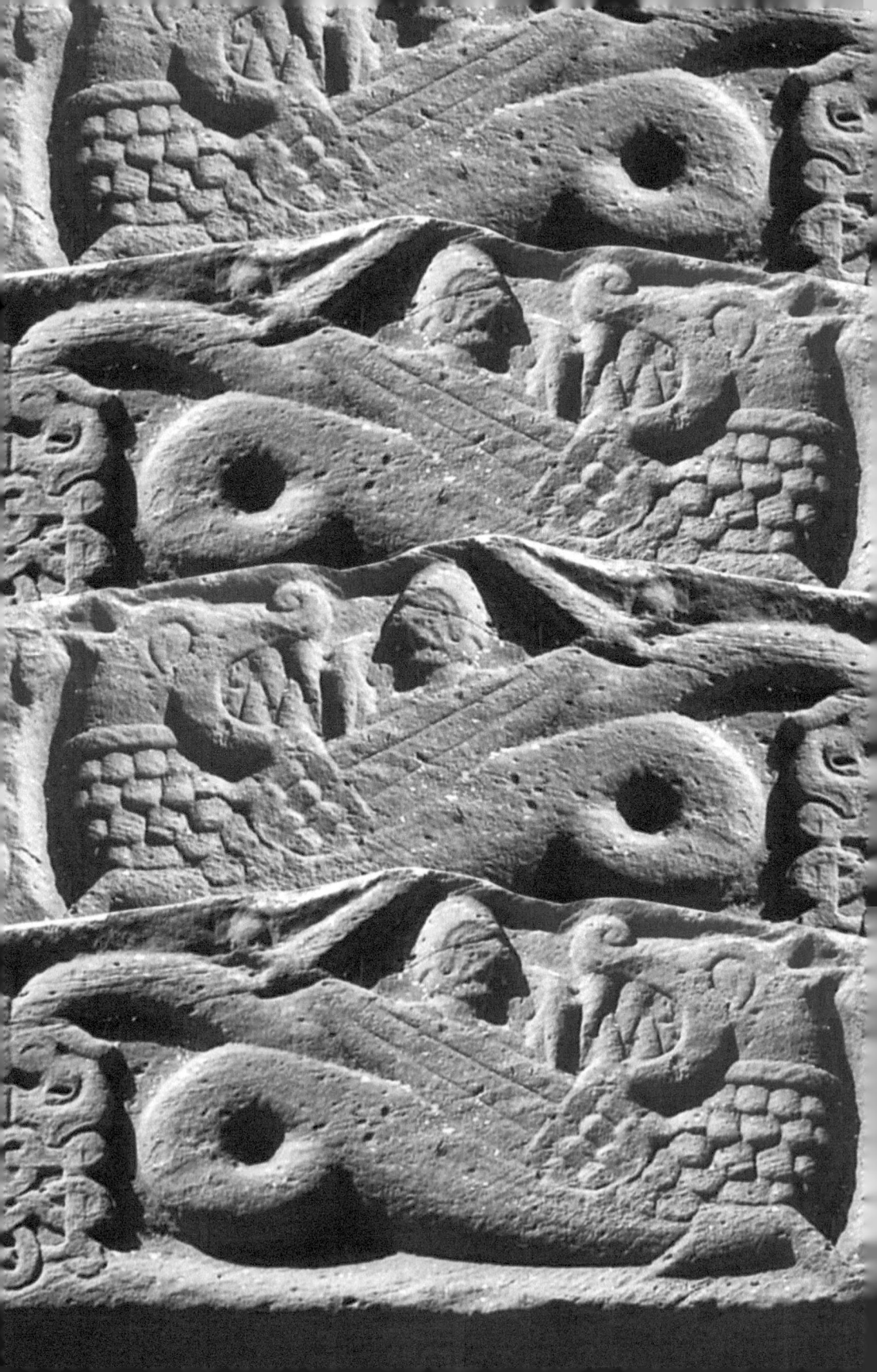

· ᚤᚤᚥ ·

A Dragon Dreamt

A dragon dreamt   in Death's manor,
A blighted barrow,   blackened by scorching,
Tending treasure   taken from kingdoms
In an olden age   when the earth was young.
Hearing this history,   a hero arrived,
Crafty Cyndraca,   the queller of ents,
Mauler of monsters   and murderer of wolves,
To break into the barrow's   black interior.
He crept carefully,   as quiet as the grave,
His cloak of darkness   keeping him hidden,
To behold a hill   of hoarded gold
And plentiful piles   of purest silver,
With starry stones   strewn through the jumble.
At the height of this heap   of hoary treasure
Were shoes that were shaped   by the shrewdest of dwarfs.
He slipped past the dragon   sleeping soundly,
And climbing to the crest   of the coveted heap,
He buckled the boots   which bore their wearer
With quickness akin   to the crack of a whip.
His feet were fast   and flashing was his blade
When he slyly slew   the sleepy dragon.
The gold he gave   to the good freemen,
For ages cursed,   their acres ravaged.

The shoes of swiftness   shot him far from there,
Like an arrow through the air—   even faster—
Over earthly   and elven lands;
Flutter your eyelids—   he has flown from sight.

· ᛪᛪᚿᛁ ·

The Queen of Ælfhám

As Dréamwulf drowsed   in a dark hollow
Under an ancient oak's   open branches,
He conjured a vision   of the Queen of Ælfhám.
Green her gloves were   and gowned in white,
She perched upon   the palest of steeds.
The Queen requested   that he kiss her lips,
And placed the poet   in a pleasing thrall;
Together they galloped   with great swiftness
Through the silent space   that separates worlds,
Their forward path   forking threefold:
The first of the roads   a route to Ósgeard,
The heavenly home   of heroes and gods;
The second way   wound to Helhám,
The gloomy gulf   which gathered the dead;
The third threaded   a thorny briar,
To a green garden   which gladdened the heart,
And Ælfhám they entered,   ever aflower.
The Queen kept him   in a castle of wonders,
A sated servant   for seven nights,
While seven years   slipped the earth by
As Dréamwulf drowsed   in a dark hollow
Under an ancient oak's   open branches.

53

· ᚢᚤᚾᛁᛁ ·

The Crow

Black my feathers   and bright my wit,
My cry is 'caw!'   and keen my beak
To maul the meat   of murder-leavings,
My claws crimson   with carrion-blood,
I dine on the dead,   a dainty treat.
My kindred crowd   when the kill is large,
A frightful family   flocking raucously
To peck and pick   at the putrid feast,
And gab gossip   in grating voices.
Of an enemy earning   our ire and spite,
I tell the tribe   and a terrible curse
Befalls this foe,   who flees the sound
Of crows calling   and keeps indoors,
The fate of fools   who offend our kind.

· ᛉᛉᚢIII ·

The Cuckoo

The cuckoo cries   the coming of spring
With a warbling wail   and a wobbling flight.
From my house on a hill   I hear his song,
Sweet as the syrup   he suckles from flowers.
Inconstant the call   the cuckoo makes,
And fleeting his favour,   a fickle bird,
Quick and crafty,   and cunning his plans,
Like lying Lúca   lavishing praise
And winning wives   with wiles and charm
To sire his sons   ere the sun arises
In another's nest,   ignoble the deed,
He flutters fast   and free of worry.

· ᛡᛡᚿᛁᛁᛁᛁ ·

The King of Cats

In a wicked wood,   where witches meet,
And ravens roost   in rowan trees,
I came across   an uncanny scene
In remote ruins,   rotted by ages:
A cavalcade of cats,   a coffin on their backs,
A crown resting   on the casket's lid,
Strode by stately,   the strangest sight.
Raving, I ran   rapidly homeward,
Where my wife wondered   at my worried looks.
I told my tale,   and Tin, my cat,
Who was sleeping soundly   by the snapping fire,
Jumped up jubilantly   and jigged on hind-legs.
'Then I am King of Cats!'   he cried with glee.
And vaulted up the chimney   to vanish evermore.

· ᚥᚥᚥ ·

The King of Nod

Aloft a lake   in the land of dreams,
Murky, murmuring   and mermaid-haunted
A ferry flew   like a fiend from Hel,
Carrying Cyndraca   across the water,
That cunning, cat-loved   curse of ettins,
To the sacred sands   of a sapphire isle.
In a crumbling castle   the King of Nod
Dwelt dismally   in this dreary place,
A rain-ravaged   wreck of masonry.
The traveller told him   tales of heroism:
Of hewing the head   of Heolstor the giant,
Of slaying a serpent   who slaughtered children,
And earning Éarendel,   the Emerald Star.
The King cackled   at Cyndraca's tales,
Listening to the legends   until late at night,
And bequeathed a cap   uncannily granting
Prophetic powers   when placed on his head.
Come the cockcrow,   the castle vanished,
And in a stone circle   stirred Cyndraca,
The coveted cap   clutched in his fingers.

· ᚤᚤᚤᛁ ·

The First Riddle

I frisk in fields   aflower with daisies,
My coat the colour   of creeping rust;
I dally till dusk;   in darkness I strike
To grasp a goose   in my greedy jaws.
I wend my way   through a wooded refuge,
The harried huntsman   hurrying after me.
Dashing and darting,   with death on my heels,
I laugh lightly   for luck remains,
And thread a thicket   of thorn with skill,
A maze the man is   too meek to enter;
Dawn arises,   and I have dodged my fate.

The Second Riddle

Madly amidst   a meadow's grass,
I leap lithely;   long my feet are.
White is my belly;   my whiskers twitch.
A herald of Hrétha,   I hop in the springtime.
By Fríg I am favoured,   her fastest runner,
Lustful, leery,   and long of ears.
Fearful of foxes,   I fly easily,
And wary of wolves,   I watch carefully.
If I meet a man,   I make my escape;
My enemies everywhere,   I earn my supper
By stealing harvests,   my strategies artful.

· ᛉᛉᛉIII ·

The Third Riddle

I screech at the sky   to scold the moon,
A dweller in darkness,   a death-omen.
My uncanny cry   causes unease;
Who hears the sound   hurries faster.
There are some who say   I am a scholar, wise,
And learnèd in lore   lost to the ages,
While others have asked   if I eat children;
Mainly my morsels   are mice and rabbits.
In Hel it's heard   I help the dead
Find their families   and fend off hounds.
The truth I'll not tell;   I betray no secrets.

The Fourth Riddle

ᚴ Cat-beloved I am,   a cunning-man,

ᛙ Yttin-hunter,   to elves a friend,

ᛏ Night-enshrouded,   a nicor-slayer,

ᛟ Dragonsbane also,   the doom of trolls,

ᚱ Rider on horseback,   the ruin of kings,

ᚠ Army-stopper,   always victorious,

ᚴ Carrier of the runesword   which conquers all,

ᚠ Am I told in song?   Do my tales resound?

· ᚠᚠᚠᚼ ·

The Fifth Riddle

Of strings I have six,   stretched from catgut
And pleasing to pluck.   The power to sway
Listeners I lend you,   and laughter I bring,
Or sudden sadness   from songs of woe.
My music makes   marvels living:
A hero from history   may howl his name
At an angry ettin,   an eater of children,
While grateful gods   are glad of the felling.
My body is built   from burnished oak;
I lie on the lap   of a lady who sings
Of love she has lost,   a lingering ghost.

The Sixth Riddle

I keep my coat   clean by licking,
And sleep in sunlight,   a soothing balm;
On padded paws   I pounce suddenly,
Serpent-slitted   my scintillating eyes.
Witches welcome me;   I walk in silence,
While rats run from me,   for rippers my claws;
Fish I favour;   I flee from water;
Cream I covet,   a cause for joy;
I purr if pet,   pleased by your stroking;
I hiss if cornered,   a haunter of darkness;
Nine my lives are,   the number of worlds.

· ᚤᚤᚤᚢᛁᛁ ·

The Seventh Riddle

Tall as towers,   our tread is long,
We carry clubs   for crushing skulls,
We eat everything,   our appetites vast,
But man is the meat   we most desire.
We thunder our threats,   three our heads are
In total or two,   betimes but one.
In bygone days,   we balanced stones
Arrayed in rings   and raised up walls.
We gall the gods,   yet give them wives,
And fee and fie   and fum our words.
Cyndraca kills us,   our kindred's bane.

· ᚢᚢᚢᚢᚢᚢ ·
The Eighth Riddle

Cold and cutting,   my coming is feared,
For none may know   the nature of my advent:
With a cat's quiet,   I creep in the dark,
Or fast, in a fury,   like a feral wolf.
I am the end of all,   the eater of gladness,
The cease of suffering   the severer of ties,
The herald of Hel,   the hero's kiss,
The scythe-swinger,   the sword's harvest,
The winter's woe,   the widow-maker;
Inevitable my advent,   yet I am ever shunned,
A lonely lord,   my law is absolute.

· ᚠᚠᚠᚢᛁᛁᛁᛁ ·

The Ninth Riddle

Ravens rally,   ready to banquet
On fallen flesh,   flayed and hanging.
The ground is groaning   from the grisly weight
Of slain soldiers,   who seep their blood
Into the earth's innards;   ever remembered
The deeds of that day,   when Death was king,
When swords were swinging,   and screams were singing,
And spears were springing,   splattering entrails,
And winged wælcyrian   welcomed the fallen
To wondrous Wælheall,   Wóden's haven,
While corpses cluttered   the crimson meadow.

· ᛉᛉᛉ ·

Mad Myrddin

Cyndraca wandered   through a Welsh forest,
Beyond the fringe   of folk he knew.
Wild this wood was   for wolves hunted,
And hares hurried   from the hoots of owls.
Here a hermit's home   he happened upon,
Where Mad Myrddin   the magus of yore,
Gave a greeting   to the grim wayfarer,
And warned that his wyrd   was winding to the day
When Hámdæl's horn   would herald the end,
Calling Cyndraca   to come and fight
In Wóden's war   waged upon ettins,
Ravens revelling   in the red murder,
And Hel hungry   for heroes' bones.

ᛏᛏᛏᛏᛁ

The Two Sisters

The two sisters strolled   beside a river,
And the darker drowned   her darling rival—
Woe befell her;   her wyrd was cruel!
Her bare bones then   a balladeer found,
Ravaged by ravens   on the river's bank;
From this morbid mound   he made a lyre,
Fitting it with fibres   of flaxen hair.
So haunting to hear,   heartbreaking the ballad
That the poet played   at the party for the wedding
Of the slain's suitor   to her deceiving murderess,
Whose loathsome lies   the lyre revealed,
And forced her to flee   to the forest of witches,
A nomad in the night,   never returning.

Birthed by a Briton

Birthed by a Briton,   bound to his father,
Cornish-cradled   Cyndraca the Saxon,
Cunning hero,   killer of giants,
Was doomed to die   in a dreaded battle;
His songs are sung   and celebrated his deeds,
His legend lingering   long since his passing.
His Cornish cousins   called him Géac,
The tart of tongue,   and tricksome of ways,
A brazen boy   who bore a pickaxe
To crack Cormoran's   uncanny skull,
The earliest exploit   of the Ettinfell.

· ᚤᚤᚤᚤᛁᛁᛁ ·

Hel Lamented

Hel lamented   to hear the news
That Heolstor's head   was hewn by a sword,
The biting blade   borne by Cyndraca,
The Ettinfell   and earl of legend.
She sent serpents   to swallow him whole,
Gruesome goblins   to grind his bones,
And tricksome trolls   to trounce him in battle.
Cyndraca conquered   the creatures she sent;
With swift swordplay   the Saxon prevailed,
Unscathed his skin,   her schemes baffled.
But Hel was heartened   to hear his wyrd:
To die on the day   of doom and horror,
Regneracu,   the raven-harvest,
The ending of all,   and overthrow of gods.

· ᚤᚤᚤᚤᛁᛁᛁᛁ ·

Lúca's Scalding

Lúca loosened   his lips to mock
The gathered gods   and give a scalding:
Brego's bravery   he brought into question,
And Fríg's faithfulness,   her freeness in love,
How Wóden walked   in a witch's guise,
And Hámdæl hated   his hallowed task;
He told Tíw then   of a traitorous wife,
And Sibb's secrets   he swore to reveal,
When Thunor threatened   to thump Lúca
On the head heavily   with his hammer's end.
Lúca left off   laughing and jeering,
And fled fleetly   in the form of a salmon
Without noticing   the net in his path,
Knotted nimbly   the night before.
Caught by his own cunning   the craven was bound,
And lashing Lúca   in a lightless cavern,
The gods gave him   a grim justice.

· ᚤᚤᚤᚢ ·

Sorrowful Sigewine

Sorrowful Sigewine   sat by her husband,
So brutally bound   with the bowels of his son,
Fateful fetters   for a feckless god.
Tirelessly truehearted,   her tears streaming,
She bore a bowl   of brass in her hands
To catch the constant   and cruel droplets
Falling from the frothing   fang of a serpent,
Poisonous punishment   for his pride and treachery.
Silently sitting   swathed in darkness
As epochs pass,   she patiently waits
For Regneracu,   the reckoning of gods,
When Lúca will be loosed,   released from his bonds,
And Sigewine's sorrows   will cease at last.

· ᚣᚣᚣᚣᚾᛁ ·

Randwulf's Return

Randwulf rode forth   through ravenous darkness
On the back of a beast,   black and wingèd,
Hurling him headlong   into horrors unknown.
The doomed and desperate   dreamer vaulted
From his monstrous mount   into measureless space,
To drift in the depths   of distant stars.
To the weary wanderer   Wóden appeared,
Astride his steed,   the stepper of worlds,
And gave guidance   through the gulf of night.
The dreamer dropped   as dawn arose,
And Randwulf reached   the refuge of his bed
In a house on a hill,   a hero's return,
A key of silver   clasped in his hand.

Dréamwulf Adrift

Dréamwulf drifted   on a distant sea,
And dreamt of dwelling   in the dale of his birth,
Of his mother's music   making him gladsome;
He sang her songs   as sleep encroached,
His frosty fingers   fluttering skillfully
O'er the length of the lyre,   alluring to hear.
The ship had sunk   and the scop was lost,
But Fríg found him   floating in the water,
And cradling his corpse,   carried him skyward
To far Folkwang,   her flowery domain,
Where the poet plays   pleasing songs for her.

· ᚢᚢᚢᚢᚾᛁᛁᛁ ·
Æon-aged Ælfflæd

Ælfflæd strummed   her strings of silver,
Lavishing listeners   with lays of old,
With moving music,   mournful and haunting,
Of lost lovers,   lies and murder,
Of crafty Cyndraca's   colourful exploits:
In the house of her heart   he held lordship.
Her wyrd was to walk   in wild despair
Beyond her years,   yearning for his notice,
Her Ettinfell,   always distant.
Deathless, doomful   and dark was the path
That æon-aged   Ælfflæd trod upon.

· ᚠᚠᚠᚢᛝᛁᛁᛁᛁ ·
Cyndraca's Wyrd

The weight of his wyrd   wearied Cyndraca,
The artful earl   and ettin-scourge,
Whose sword's sharpness   all substance cut,
Whose uncanny cloak   kept him hidden,
Whose cap uncovered   coveted secrets,
Whose boots bolted him   in the blink of an eye.
His boons brought him   abundant fame,
But love eluded   the forlorn warrior,
His triumphs taking   a toll on his soul.
On the edge of ice   at the end of the world,
A raven roosted   on a rocky cliff
To call Cyndraca   the cunning man
To Regneracu,   the wreck of worlds,
Wóden's wassail,   the war in dreams.

ᛁ

A Wheel of Ravens

A wheel of ravens   revelled loudly
Over a bitter battle   of bold warriors
Who lost their lives   and lay in mud,
A feast of flesh   for the frenzied birds.
Endless ettins   the earl slaughtered there,
Valiant Cyndraca,   killer of giants;
At the swing of a sword,   seven tumbled!
The elder gods   that evening perished:
By a wolf's gnawing   did Wóden die,
A fang's venom   was the fall of Thunor,
Lúca relinquished   his life to Hámdæl.
Cyndraca escaped,   by his cloak hidden,
Guided by a lantern   engraved with runes,
A weary wanderer,   wyrd-eluding,
Deemed undying,   dark his path was.

Hræfna hwéol   hludlic plægde
Ofer bitere beadu   bealdra drenga,
Hwa hiera lif forlosedon   ond lágon in fenne,
Flǽsces fréolsung   fuglum wódum.
Endeléase eotenas   se eorl þǽr slóg,
Þrǽcróf Cyndraca   þyrsa bana;
Sweordes swenge   seofon féollon!
Þá ealde ése   þæm ǽfenne druron:
In wulfes céacum   Wóden diegede,
Þunres fell wæs   fængtóþes átor,
His lif Lúca   forlosede Hámdæle.
Cyndraca befléag   casule gedíeglod,
Lǽded leohtfǽte   beleged rúnum,
Wérig wídfarend   wyrd fléogende,
Gedémed undéadlíc,   deorc his pæþ wæs.

ᚢᚱᚨᚾᛏᚨ · ᚾᚹᛖᛗᛏ · ᚾᛚᛏᛞᚷᛁᛚ · ᛚᛚᚨᚷᛞᛗ

ᚠᚹᛖᚱ · ᛒᛁᛏᛖᚱᛖ · ᛒᛗᛖᛞᛞ · ᛒᛗᛖᛏᛞᚱᚨ · ᛞᚱᛖᛁᚷᚨ

ᚾᚢᚨ · ᚾᛁᛖᚱᚨ · ᛚᛁᚹ · ᚹᚹᚱᛚᚢᛗᛞᚨᛏ · ᚨᛏᛞ · ᛚᛚᚷᚨᛏ · ᛁᛏ · ᚹᛖᛏᛏᛖ

ᚹᛚᚨᚢᛚᛖᛞ · ᚦᚹᛖᛖᚱᛚᛏᚷ · ᚹᛞᚷᛚᛞᛖ · ᚹᚹᛞᛞᛖ

ᛖᛏᛞᛖᛚᛖᚹᛖ · ᛗᛖᛏᛖᛖᛞ · ᛖᛗ · ᛗᚹᚱᛚ · ᚦᚨᚱ · ᛚᛚᚨᚷ

ᚦᚱᚨᛚᚱᚹ · ᛚᛞᛏᛞᚱᛖᛚ · ᚦᛞᚱᛖᛖ · ᛒᚨᛏᚨ

ᛚᚹᛖᚱᛞᛞᛖ · ᛚᚹᛖᛏᚷᛖ · ᛚᛗᛖᚹᚹᛏ · ᚹᛖᛖᛚᛚᛏ

ᚦᚨ · ᛗᛖᛏᛞᛖ · ᛗᛖᛖ · ᚦᛖᛖ · ᚹᚹᛖᛏᛏᛖ · ᛞᚱᚢᚱᚨᛏ

ᛁᛏ · ᚢᛚᚹᛖᛖ · ᛚᛗᛖᛚᚢᛖ · ᚹᚹᛞᛖᛏ · ᛞᛁᛖᚷᛖᛞᛞ

ᚦᛏᚱᛖᛖ · ᚹᛖᛚᛚ · ᚨᚹᛖ · ᚹᚨᛏᚷᛏᚦᛖᛖ · ᛚᛚᚨᚱ

ᚾᛁᛖ · ᛚᛁᚹ · ᛚᛚᛚᚨ · ᚹᚹᚱᛚᛖᛖᛞᛞ · ᚾᛖᛗᛞᛖᛚᛖ

ᛚᛞᛏᛞᚱᛖᛚᚨ · ᛒᛖᚹᛚᛖᚷ · ᛚᚨᚹᚢᛚᛖ · ᚷᛖᛞᛁᛗᚷᛚᛖᛞ

ᛚᛏᛞᛗᛖ · ᛚᛗᛖᛏᚾᚹᚱᛏᛖ · ᛒᛖᛚᚷᛗᛞ · ᚱᛏᚢᛗ

ᚹᛗᚱᛁᚷ · ᚹᛁᛞᚹᚱᛖᛗᛏᛞ · ᚦᛞᚱᛞ · ᚹᛚᛖᚷᛗᛏᛞᛗ

ᚷᛗᛞᛗᛗᛗᛞ · ᚾᛏᛞᛗᛖᛞᚷᛁᛚ · ᛞᛗᛖᚱᛚ · ᚾᛁᛖ · ᛚᛚᚦ · ᚹᛖᛖ

The Lay of Géac Ettinfell

1.

Now to my lyre, listen,   and learn the tale
Of artful Géac,   the Ettinfell,
A Hel-harrower,   a hero like Thunor
And wise as Wóden,   his wit quick-fire.
In a wild woodland   his war began:
A fearful fox   fleeing Géac,
His lantern's light   leaping harelike.
His heart leapt too   as he hurried to the cave
To set a snare   with a serpent's craft.
Delving deeply,   he dug a pit,
Careful to cover it   with a carpet of sticks,
And, hefting his horn,   he heartily blew.
An ettin awoke,   angered by the bedlam,
With staggering steps   to stumble out
And fast falling   into the fateful trap.
Géac jeered then   at the giant's plight,
And pointed a pick-axe   to pelt his head
With bloody blows   that broke his skull.
Joyful was Géac!   The giant was dead,
His efforts earning him   ageless renown.

2.

On a journey to find   more giants to kill,
His heart happy,   with hands on his belt,
By a fountain Géac   fell into slumbers,
Then, snatched suddenly   by a snarling ettin,
Was carried to a castle   of crumbling stone,
Bones on the bulwarks,   boding evil.
Locking Géac there,   the loathly ent
Fetched a kinsman   for a foul supper.
Mournful moaning   emerged from the darkness:
Women wailing   warnings to Géac
To flee as far   and fast as he could.
But, daring and doughty,   dauntless was Géac:
Eager to end   his enemies' lives.
Tying two nooses   tightly together,
He ringed the ropes   around their necks,
The other ends   over a rafter,
And throttled the ettins,   a thrill in his blood.
In a dark dungeon   the damsels he'd heard
Were thin from starving,   three in number,
From hooks hanging   by their hair and wretched.
Géac loosed them,   and, lulling their fears,
Led them to liberty,   his luck boundless.

3.

Wandering to Wales next,   the wayfarer tired
And looked for lodging   at a lonesome manor.
A towering, terrible,   two-headed ettin
Ushered him in   and offered a room,
Muttering of the morsel   he'd make of Géac,
Clubbing him crudely   and killing him in bed.
Géac smirked at that   and swore otherwise.
In the bed's blanket   a billet he laid,
And crouched quietly   in a corner in the dark.
The ettin entered   at early morning,
Battering the billet   with blows from his club,
And, with a lively laugh,   left for breakfast.
Jolly was Géac   when he joined his host,
Saying how soundly   he'd slept that night
But for the tickling tail   of a tiny rat.
The ettin then offered   an oversized bowl
Of poorly prepared   porridge to eat.
First placing a pouch   for the pitiful mush
In his shirt shrewdly   to shovel it therein,
Géac slit next   the sack he'd hidden
And the porridge poured   pattering downwards.
The jealous giant   jeered at the mischief,

And crowing that he, too,   could cut his belly,
He stupidly stabbed   his own stomach and died,
Earning Géac   an added triumph:
In nurseries his name   would never be forgot.

4.

An ætheling came   one autumn to Wales,
For at home he'd heard   the horrible news
Of a lovely lady   lowered by demons,
And vehemently vowed   to vanquish them all.
Midday at market   he met with a rabble
Hindering the headway   to hallowed ground
Of a dead debtor,   bedevilling his rest.
Pity this prince took   and paid the merchants,
Which left his leather   lacking silver.
Géac noticed   this noble deed
And offered aid   to the innocent prince.
They came to a castle,   the keep of a giant
Who was three-headed,   his hair like flame.
'The King is close-by!'   called Géac to him,
'A thousand men,   thirsting for blood!'
'Then hurry! Hide me!'   howled the giant.

'Lay me and lock me   in this lightless vault.'
Géac chuckled,   cheerfully obeying,
And made merry   with his master that night
In the ettin's hall,   emptying the larder,
Raising a rumpus   and raiding the coffers.
Later the giant   lavished gratitude,
And furnished Géac   with four armaments:
A singing sword   which sundered all matter,
A cloak of concealment,   conjuring obscurity,
Boots which bore one   in the blink of an eye,
And a cognizant cap,   counsel unerring.
So equipped, Géac   escorted the prince
To the haunted hall   of the haughty lady.
Welcoming the wayfarers   to her wintry keep,
The lady served lamb   and laughed wickedly,
Ordering the ætheling   to unearth her handkerchief
By daybreak or die—   a dastardly errand.
Géac's cap soon   uncovered the secret,
And, shoes speeding him,   enshrouded by the cloak,
To Hel he hastened   where the handkerchief lay.
A new labour   the lady decreed:
The prince must expose   who planted a kiss on her
Over the night,   or else he would die.
Well, the lady's lips   had with Lúca's met,

And Géac's sword   severed the head
Of the Lord of Lies,   loosing his hold
And ending his evil   influence on her wishes.

5.

Earning the epithet   of Ettinfell,
Géac tasted   triumphs aplenty:
The two-fold throats   of Thunderdell no hurdle,
Nor Nimrod's nose;   never failing,
He slew giants   with a jaunty air,
Their heads carted   to the King as gifts.
His final foes were   a foul enchanter
And an ugly ettin,   acolytes together,
Roosting repugnantly   in a ruined tower
Guarded by griffins   growling in fetters.
His cloak covering him   to keep unseen,
Géac evaded   the eyes of the beasts,
And happened on a horn   which hung from a chain,
Like Hámdæl's horn,   heavy with portent.
Etched underneath   were ominous words:
Be bold, be bold,   and blow this horn,
To banish the night   and bring the dawn.

Sounding the signal   and smiting the ettin
Géac satiated   his sword with blood.
The alchemist abdicated,   his art undone,
And a distressed damsel,   the daughter of a thane,
Was freed from the form   of a four-legged hind.
Géac was elevated   to earl by the King,
And merrily married   the maiden he'd freed.
His songs are sung   unceasingly now,
Raucously roared   and rousing gladness.

GLOSSARY

[Note: Rather than use IPA notation, I have tried to make the pronunciations as accessible to a general audience as possible. The pronunciation of the letter 'y' in Old English does not have an exact equivalent in Modern English, but is like the German 'ü', a sound like the 'ee' in 'see' said with rounded lips.]

Ælfhám. Pronounced 'ălf-hahm'. Elfland. The abode of the elves. (Old Norse *Álfheimr*)

Ælfflæd. Pronounced 'ălf-lăd'. An Old English woman's name meaning elf-beauty.

Ætheling. Pronounced 'ăth-eh-ling'. A prince.

Ángnesboda. Pronounced 'ahn-yes-boh-dah'. A giantess and mother of Eormenwyrm, the world-serpent. Her name means sorrow-bringer. *Angrboða* in Old Norse.

Bældæg. Pronounced 'băl-die'. A much loved god who falls foul of Lúca's treachery. *Baldr* in Old Norse.

Brego. A speculative Old English name for the poet-god called *Bragi* in Old Norse. His name means lord or chief.

Brósingamene. Pronounced 'broh-sing-ah-meh-neh'. The Old English name for the legendary necklace *Brísingamen*. Attested in *Beowulf*.

Cormoran. A giant in Cornish legend.

Cyndraca. Pronounced 'CÜN-dra-ca'. The precise meaning of this name is uncertain. *Draca* is Old English for dragon or wyrm. *Cyn* could be either a shortening of *cynn* (kin) or *cyne* (kingly). One theory holds that the name means 'kin to the Devil', which would suggest an early Christian influence.

Defenascír. Pronounced 'dev-en-ah-sheer'. The Old English name for the county of Devon.

Dréamwulf. Pronounced 'dray-am-wulf'. *Dréam* is the Old English word for song, not dream, making the name particularly apt for a *scop*.

Éarendel. Pronounced 'ay-ar-en-del'. The Old English name for the morning star. This word has been extolled for its especial beauty.

Earl. From the Old English *eorl*. While the word can denote a high-ranking status, it can also mean hero.

Ent. An alternate Old English word for *eoten*, a giant. Although ents are now popularly thought of as trees due to the works of J. R. R. Tolkien, they were simply giants in Anglo-Saxon belief. The word is referenced in the Old English poem *The Wanderer* in which toppled ruins are referred to as *eald enta geweorc*: the ancient work of giants.

Eormenwyrm. Pronounced 'eh-or-men-würm'. The world-girding serpent and nemesis of Thunor. *Jörmungandr* in Old Norse.

Ettin. A later form of the Old English *eoten*, the equivalent of the Old Norse *jötunn*, one of the primary antagonists of the gods. Traditionally translated as giant, there is some contention over this interpretation. Nevertheless, there are ample references indicating that *eotenas* were of great size: for example, an *eotenisc* sword in *Beowulf* was too large for an ordinary man to wield and the glove of the *jötunn* Skrýmir was mistaken for a house.

Ettinfell. From the Old English *eoten* (giant) and *fell* (ruin, death, doom); a kenning for giant-killer. There is an elaborate kenning for Thor in Norse skaldic poetry, *felli fjörnets goða flugstalla*: feller of the life-webs of the gods of the flight edges; i.e. giant-killer.

Folkwang. The name of Fríg's heavenly field, where half of the favoured dead will reside after death. *Fólkvangr* in Old Norse.

Fríg. Pronounced 'free'. The Old English name for either the Norse goddess Freyja or Frigg. It is speculated that the two were once the same entity. In my poetry, I depict Fríg as having Freyja's qualities.

Géac. Pronounced 'yay-ack'. An Old English man's name, from a word meaning cuckoo. A later spelling of the same name was recorded as 'Iac', and as the distinction between 'i' and 'j' in mediæval English is mutable, it must be noted that the name bears a striking resemblance to the modern English 'Jack', whose giant-killing exploits are well known.

Hámdæl. Pronounced 'hahm-dăl' The watchman of the gods. *Heimdallr* in Old Norse.

Hel. The abode of the dead (also called Helhám) and the

name of its ruling goddess.

Heolstor. Pronounced 'heh-ol-stor'. The name of this Hel-ettin means darkness in Old English.

Hréam. Pronounced 'hray-am'. The Old English name for the ettin-king known as *Þrymr* in Old Norse.

Hrétha (*Hréþe*). An early English goddess who sole attribution comes the late 7th- and early 8th-century monk and scholar, the Venerable Bede. On the Anglo-Saxon calendar, her month was called *Hréþmónaþ*, which was roughly equivalent to March, when sacrifices were made to her. *Éostermónaþ* (April) was similarly named for the goddess Éostre.

Hyge. Pronounced 'hü-yeh'. One of Wóden's two ravens. *Hyge* and *Myne* are the Old English words for the Old Norse *Huginn* and *Muninn*, meaning Thought and Memory.

Lay. A poem or song. From the Old English *léoð*.

Lúca. Pronounced 'loo-ka' ('oo' as in 'moon'). The reconstructed Old English name for the god known to the Norse as Loki. He is not attested in Old English writing, but Loki's presence is so pervasive in the Norse myths, I am persuaded that he was known by at least some of the early English, for who doesn't like a good trickster tale?

Middangeard. Pronounced 'mid-dan-yard'. The Old English name for the Earth (as opposed to other realms such as Ósgeard or Hel). *Miðgarðr*, in Old Norse. Often translated as Middle-Earth.

Móna. The moon-god.

Myrddin. The legendary Welsh bard and magician later known as Merlin.

Nicor. A water-monster.

Ósgeard. Pronounced 'oz-yard'. The abode of the gods. Also a man's name listed in the Domesday Book. *Ásgarðr* in Old Norse.

Púca. A goblin or mischievous spirit. In later English called a puck.

Rán. Also *Rán* in Old Norse. The goddess and personification of the sea. The name means robbery, for she robs men of their lives. She is the wife of the sea god Éagor (*Ægir* in Old Norse).

Randwulf. An Old English name meaning 'shield-wolf'. Randolph in modern English.

Regneracu. Pronounced 'ren-yer-a-coo'. The reconstructed Old English name for the great battle that brings about the fall of the gods. *Ragnarök* in Old Norse.

Scop. Pronounced 'shop'. A poet. Composer and reciter of traditional Old English verse. Equivalent to the Old Norse *skáld*.

Scopcræft. Pronounced 'shop-cræft'. Poetry. The poet's art.

Sibb. The golden-haired wife of Thunor. *Sif* in Old Norse. Her name means kinship, love or peace.

Sigewine. Pronounced 'sih-yeh-win-eh'. The wife of Lúca. Her Old Norse name is *Sigyn*.

Sunne. Pronounced 'sun-neh'. The sun-goddess.

Thunor (Þunor). Pronounced 'thoon-or' ('oo' as in 'book'). The Old English name for the god Thor (Old Norse *Þórr*). His name means thunder.

Tíw. Pronounced 'tee-oo' ('oo' as in 'moon'). The god

who sacrificed a hand to bind the Fen-wolf. *Týr* in Old Norse.

Vampyre. The word "vampyre" does not enter the English language until 1734, but a possible Old English equivalent is *þyrs* (thyrs). Often translated as monster or giant, the word may derive from the same root as "thirst," which is certainly suggestive of a vampire. It was Jacob Grimm who first noted the vampiric qualities of Grendel in the Old English poem *Beowulf*: Grendel is a *sceadugenga* (shadow-walker) who *com on wanre niht* (came in the dark night) and *blod edrum dranc* (drank blood from veins).

Wælcyrie. Pronounced 'wăl-kü-ree'. The Old English word for valkyrie (Old Norse *valkyrja*). Plural *wælcyrian*.

Wælheall. Pronounced 'wăl-hal'. The hall of the slain. *Valhǫll* in Old Norse. Commonly called Valhalla.

Wícing. Pronounced 'weech-ing'. Viking. An Old Norse-speaking seafarer who raided the eastern coast of England.

Wínland. Pronounced 'ween-land'. Old English for Vinland, a section of coastal North America explored and briefly settled by Vikings.

Winterfylleth (Ƿinterfylleþ). Pronounced 'win-ter-fü-leth'. The first full moon in October, considered to be the start of winter in early mediæval England.

Wóden. Pronounced 'woh-den'. The Old English name for the god Odin (Old Norse *Óðinn*).

Wódnesmeolc. Pronounced 'wohd-nes-meh-olc'. Wóden's milk. Another name for the Mead of Poetry.

Wyrd. Pronounced 'würd'. Fate, something which was considered inescapable by the early English, and held an important place in their beliefs.

Wyrd Sisters. In Norse mythology, one's fate was decided by the Norns, three sisters whose names were *Urðr*, *Verðandi* and *Skuld*. These figures recur in English folklore as three prophetic witches like the ones depicted in Shakespeare's *Macbeth*.

Wyrm. Pronounced 'würm'. A large serpent or dragon. Used interchangeably with the Old English word *draca*.

Yttin. An alternate spelling of ettin.

Riddle Answers

The First Riddle .... A fox

The Second Riddle .... A hare

The Third Riddle .... An owl

The Fourth Riddle .... Cyndraca

The Fifth Riddle .... A lyre

The Sixth Riddle .... A cat

The Seventh Riddle .... Ettins

The Eighth Riddle .... Death

The Ninth Riddle .... A battlefield

An Analysis of "The Cuckoo"

The cuckoo cries   the coming of spring
With a warbling wail   and a wobbling flight.
From my house on a hill,   I hear his song,
Sweet as the syrup   he suckles from blooms.
Inconstant the call   the cuckoo makes,
Fleeting his favour,   a fickle bird,
Quick and crafty,   and cunning his plans,
Lying like Lúca,   lavishing honey
And wooing wives   with wiles and charm
To sire his sons   ere the sun appears
In another's nest,   ignoble the deed,
He flutters fast   and free of care.

The | **CUCK** | oo | **CRIES**   the | **COM** | ing of | ***SPRING***
With a | **WARB** | ling | **WAIL**   and a | **WOB** | bling | ***FLIGHT***.
From my | **HOUSE** | on a | **HILL**,   I | **HEAR** | his | ***SONG***,
SWEET | as the | **SYR** | up   he | **SUCK** | les from | ***BLOOMS***.
In | **CON** | stant the | **CALL**   the | **CUCK** | oo | ***MAKES***,
FLEET | ing his | **FA** | vour,   a | **FICK** | le | ***BIRD***,
QUICK | and | **CRAF** | ty,   and | **CUN** | ning his | ***PLANS***,
LY | ing like | **LU** | ca,   **LAV** | ish ing | **HON** | ey
And | **WOO** | ing | **WIVES**   with | **WILES** | and | ***CHARM***
To | **SIRE** | his | **SONS**   ere the | **SUN** | ap | ***PEARS***
In a | **NOTH** | er's | **NEST**,   ig | **NO** | ble the | ***DEED***,
He | **FLUT** | ters | **FAST**   and | **FREE** | of | ***CARE***.

[Note: Each half-line must have four metrical positions. There are two strongly stressed syllables in each half-line. Only one stressed syllable can occupy a single metrical position, but consecutive unstressed syllables combine into one position. One or both stressed syllables in the first half-line must alliterate (in bold). The first stressed syllable in the second half-line alliterates with the others (in bold), but the second stressed syllable in the second half-line must not alliterate (bolded and in italics).]

A Note on the Numbering of the Poems

In an 11th-century manuscript kept at Cambridge University (Corpus Christi College, MS 041), there is an example of runes being substituted for Roman numerals: **XII** is written as ᛏ‖ and **XXX** as ᛏᛏᛏ. I extrapolated that the rune ᚾ could take the place of the Roman numeral **V** and ᚱ represent **L**, and whimsically adopted this system myself.

Image Credits

Title page spread: Photomontage by Dan Sauer, making use of an image of the reconstruction of the lyre from the Sutton Hoo ship-burial 1, Suffolk (England). Lyre reconstruction by Messers Dolmetsch. Photograph by Steven J. Plunkett, 2007. Used under the Creative Commons Attribution-Share Alike 2.5 Generic license. Lyre image has been modified from its original form. Photomontage copyright © 2023 by Daniel V. Sauer.

Contents spread: Photomontage by Dan Sauer from public domain materials, copyright © 2023 by Daniel V. Sauer.

Image facing page 1: Buckle found in an Anglo-Saxon cemetery at Finglesham, Kent. On display at the Ashmolean Museum. Photo by Ethan Doyle White (Doyle of London). Used under the Creative Commons Attribution-Share Alike 4.0 International License. Modified to remove background and improve contrast.

Image on page 10: Captioned as "The Bound Devil. Kirkby Stephen." The stone features a depiction of a bound, horned figure, sometimes theorized as the Norse deity Loki. Source: *Notes on the Early Sculptured Cross* by William Slater Calverly, 1899. Public Domain.

Image on page 18: Seax of Beagnoth, on display at the British Museum. Photo by BabelStone. Image used under the Creative Commons Attribution-Share Alike 3.0 Unported license. Modified to remove background and repeat image.

Image on page 21: Public domain.

Image on page 24: Freja Brisingamen (Viking age). Photo courtesy of Statens Histariska Museum. Used under the Creative Commons Attribution 2.5 Generic license. Modified to remove background and improve contrast.

Image on page 30: Early Anglo-Saxon era silver-gilt plated disc brooch, 6th to 7th century AD. Photo courtesy of Trustees of the British Museum. Used under the Creative Commons Attribution-Share Alike 4.0 International License. Modified to remove background and improve contrast.

Images on pages 34, 38 and 78: Parts of the Gosforth Cross. Engraved reproduction, published in 1913. Public domain. Modified to remove background and/or repeat image.

Image on page 42: The St. Cuthbert Gospel of St. John; the oldest intact European book. Photo courtesy of the British Library. Used under the Creative commons CC0 1.0 Universal Public Domain Dedication.

Image on page 46: A helmet plate patris, from the article "Helmets and Swords in Beovulf" by Knut Stjerna, 1903. Public domain.

Image on page 50: St. Bees Dragon Stone. Romanesque lintel, Ca. 1120 AD. Photo by Doug Sim. Used under the Creative Commons Attribution-Share Alike 3.0 Unported license. Modified to remove background and repeat image.

Image on page 54: Shield ornament from the Sutton Hoo burial, British Museum. Photo by Johnbod, 2010. Used under the Creative Commons Attribution-Share Alike 3.0 Unported license. Modified to remove background and improve contrast.

Image on page 58: Gerhard Munthe (1849-1929). Illustration for Ynglingesaga. Snorre 1899 edition. Public domain.

Image on page 62: Owl miniature from the Aberdeen Bestiary. 12th century. Public domain.

Image on page 66: Peterborough Cat. Peterborough Psalter and Bestiary. Ca. 13th century. Public domain.

Image on page 66: A valkyrie and raven having a conversation. Illustration for "Harals Harfagr" in the magazine *Once a Week*, 1862. Woodcut engraved by Joseph Swain from art by Frederick Sandys. Public domain.

Images on pages 74, 88 and 95: Illustrations by Richard Doyle (1824-1883) from *Jack and the Giants*, 1851. Public domain.

Image on page 84: Ragnarok. Illustration by Johannes Gehrts (1855-1921). Public domain.

Any modifications to the images above are copyright © 2023 by Daniel V. Sauer.

Acknowledgements

I am profoundly grateful to Dr. Dennis Wise for first sparking my interest in this poetic form with an invitation to submit to his anthology, *Speculative Poetry and the Modern Alliterative Revival* (Fairleigh Dickinson University Press, 2023), the first place "The Lay of Géac Ettinfell" was published. His patience was inexhaustible in answering all my questions about the mechanics of alliterative verse and in editing my first attempts at its composition. Without him, this book would not exist.

"The Ninth Riddle" (as "The Battlefield") was published in *Spectral Realms* No. 19, Hippocampus Press, 2023.

"The Vampyre of the Fens" was published in *The Vampiricon: Imaginings & Images of the Vampire*, Mind's Eye Publications, 2023

"Randwulf's Return" was published in *For the Outsider: Poems Inspired by H. P. Lovecraft*, Hippocampus Press, 2023.

"The Song of the Sword" was published in *Spectral Realms* No. 18, Hippocampus Press, 2023.

"Mother's Night" was published in *Eternal Haunted Summer*, Winter Solstice 2021, 2021 and *The Best of Eternal Haunted Summer: A Thirteenth Anniversary Edition*, 2023.

"Heolstor" was published in *Spectral Realms* No. 17, Hippocampus Press, 2022.

"The Eighth Riddle" (as "The Riddle") was published in *What Remains*, Firbolg Publishing, 2022.

"The King of Cats" was published in *Spectral Realms* No. 16, Hippocampus Press, 2022.

About the Contributors

ADAM BOLIVAR is a formal poet of dark fantasy, a weird fiction writer and a playwright for marionettes with a particular interest in balladry, alliterative verse and "Jack" tales. He is the author of *The Lay of Old Hex* (Hippocampus Press, 2017), *The Ettinfell of Beacon Hill* (Jackanapes Press, 2021) and *Ballads for the Witching Hour* (Hippocampus Press 2022). A second volume of his occult detective *Ettinfell* saga is due out from Jackanapes Press in 2024 and third is forthcoming. A marionette-maker, he has written and performed in several original marionette plays performed by puppet troupes in Boston, Berkeley, Portland and Salem, Oregon. A native of gambrel-roofed Boston, Massachusetts, he now resides in the gloomy dreamlands of Portland, Oregon with his golden-haired wife and son.

adambolivar.com

DENNIS WILSON WISE is a professor of practice at the University of Arizona where he also serves as the English Department's Director of Undergraduate Studies. His research focuses mainly on epic fantasy, Tolkien in particular, and his work has appeared in *Tolkien Studies*, *Law & Literature*, *Journal of the Fantastic in the Arts*, *Gothic Studies*, *Extrapolation*, *English Text Construction*, and more. In 2019 Wise received a R. D. Mullen Postdoctoral Fellowship from *Science Fiction Studies* to help support archival research into modern alliterative poetry. He has also earned awards for his teaching and his research alike, including the SFRA's Mary Kay Bray Award in 2023, and Wise was the reviews editor for *Fafnir: Nordic Journal of SFF Research* when it became the first academic journal to ever win a World Fantasy Award.

"...Bolivar's tales of supernatural investigator John Drake are frightening, whimsical, adventurous, and above all else, thoroughly entertaining! ...somewhere between Seabury Quinn's Jules de Grandin and Manly Wade Wellman's Silver John."

—PETER RAWLIK, Author of *The Miskatonic University Spiritualism Club*

THE ETTINFELL OF BEACON HILL
GOTHIC TALES OF BOSTON
BY ADAM BOLIVAR

ILLUSTRATED BY DAN SAUER

From the author of *The Lay of Old Hex: Spectral Ballads and Weird Jack Tales*—

With the sword of Jack the Giant-killer at his side, John Drake stalks the streets of 1920s Boston, fulfilling his ancestor's compact to protect the city from eldritch incursions...

AVAILABLE NOW!

JACKANAPES PRESS

www.JackanapesPress.com
www.facebook.com/Jackanapes-Press

"...spirited paeans to the Season of the Pumpkin."
—K. A. Opperman, author of *Past the Glad and Sunlit Season*

A DARK CELEBRATION OF
HALLOWEEN & FOLK HORROR

SCOTT J. COUTURIER has distinguished himself with poems of uncanny beauty and dread, appearing in the pages of *Spectral Realms*, *The Audient Void*, *Eternal Haunted Summer*, and other journals of the Weird. His poems are singularly sensitive to the darker aspects of nature. Jackanapes Press is pleased to offer *I Awaken in October*—Couturier's first volume of poetry—which collects a cornucopia of seasonal horrors and autumnal delights. Follow the path to Summer's end, where the last gold-litten days malinger into cobweb; where gleaming trails of jack-o-lanterns light the way; where Queen Mab and Cernunnos reign.

"Let me reveal something about *I Awaken In October*.
It's not just a book of dark, uncanny folk poems—it's a portal.
And through it we perceive again, we course-correct the psyche.
A brilliant, haunting collection that bridges the gap."

—Jay Sturner, naturalist and author of *The Hunchback's Captive and Others*

AVAILABLE NOW FROM

www.JackanapesPress.com
www.facebook.com/Jackanapes-Press

NOT A PRINCESS

BUT (YES) THERE WAS A PEA

& OTHER FAIRY TALES TO FOMENT REVOLUTION

REBECCA BUCHANAN

"A brilliant collection

exploring the darkest sides of humanity through a fairy tale lens, *Not a Princess* leads you down a memory lane paved with gilded bones and bloody stones. Lyrically and viscerally marrying feminist, social, and environmental horror, Rebecca Buchanan's crafty cats, weary wolves, and disgruntled daughters will captivate you with razor-sharp verses and sumptuously twisted imagery. A perfect stormy evening read."

—JESSICA McHUGH, Bram Stoker & Elgin Award nominated author of *A Complex Accident of Life*

What if the Sleeping Beauty left to make her own life? What if Bluebeard's wife seized the opportunity for justice? What if the witch truly loved Rapunzel? What if Snow White learned the virtues of right rulership from the dwarves, and Jack learned wisdom from the giants?

DIG DEEPER. TWIST THE TALES AROUND.
FAIRY TALES ARE REVOLUTIONARY.

Illustrated throughout with classic art by Harry Clarke, Walter Crane, Gustave Doré, Albrecht Dürer and others.

AVAILABLE NOW FROM

JACKANAPES PRESS

www.JackanapesPress.com

www.facebook.com/Jackanapes-Press

FROM THE AUTHOR OF THE WITHERING

A Tor Nightfire selection for 10 Best Horror Poetry Collections of 2020

RENOWNED HORROR POET ASHLEY DIOSES SHOWS US THE TWISTED ROOTS AT THE VERY HEART OF HER BLEAK AND MACABRE VISION

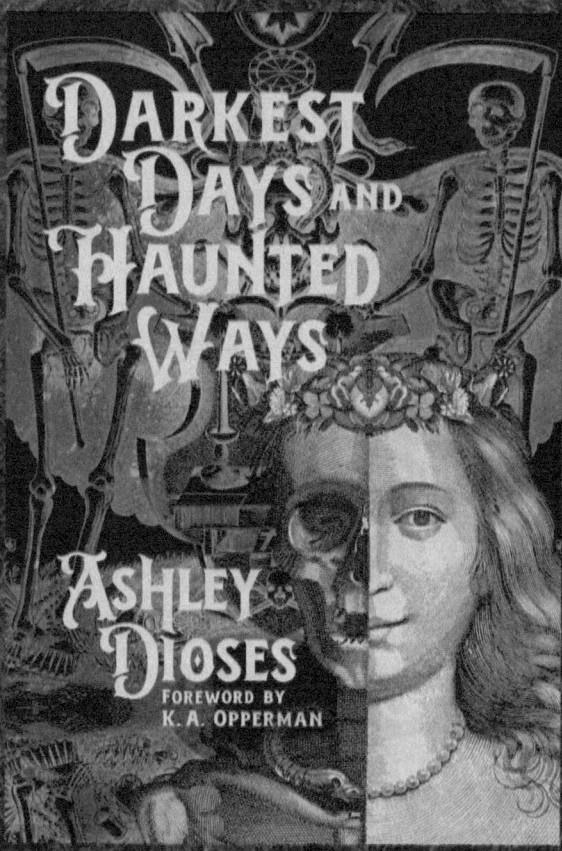

Once meant for inclusion with the rest of her formative work in *The Withering* but omitted for stylistic reasons, these poems attain a doomful thematic cohesion all their own. Written between the ages of fourteen and seventeen, but now polished by an experienced hand, these poems directly reflect—as in a cold, cracked mirror—the angst and emotional turmoil that informed those years of her life. With the publication of this book, these macabre paeans and lamentations of the damned take their rightful place beside *The Withering* as its indispensable companion volume.

"*Darkest Days and Haunted Ways* is sensuous and sensual, grim and madly gay. It evokes primal, hungry rites, and recalls the half-forgotten myths of an ancient feminine who is to be both feared and desired. These poems are the mutterings of a witch-woman deep in her cave, wrapped in bones and roots as she listens to the whisperings of worms. Discomfiting, disturbing, galvanizing, and startling."

— REBECCA BUCHANAN, author of *Not a Princess, But (Yes) There Was a Pea and Other Poems to Foment Revolution*

AVAILABLE NOW!

www.JackanapesPress.com

www.facebook.com/Jackanapes-Press

www.ingramcontent.com/pod-product-compliance
Lightning Source LLC
Chambersburg PA
CBHW021649120626
46545CB00002B/775